Three Men Who Walked in Fire

DANIEL 3 FOR CHILDREN

Written by Joann Schock
Illustrated by Sally Mathews

Concordia Publishing House

ARCH Books

One day in old Jerusalem
three little boys ran fast.
They hid and watched while soldiers armed
with swords and spears marched past.
"Burn down the houses! Steal the gold!"
they heard the soldiers shout.
The boys crouched very quietly,
not daring to look out.

But soon a soldier saw them there.
He quickly caught all three.

"You boys will make good slaves," he said.
"I'll take you home with me."

Though they were slaves for many years,
the boys did not despair.
"Dear God, we know You're by our side,"
they said each day in prayer.

The oldest was the smartest one—
they called him wise Shadrach.
The youngest was the strongest one—
no one could beat Meshach.
The third was liked the best of all—
no matter where he went,
Abednego brought fun and grins
and laughing merriment.

One day the king of this strange land was feeling very proud.

He thought about how great he was
until he said aloud,
"There's really nothing in the world
I cannot do or say.
Why, I could even make a god!
I'll do it right away."

"Go out," the king called to his men,
"and gather all the gold."
The soldiers quickly hurried off
to do as they were told.

One morning near the city walls
the people saw a sight
so horrible to look upon
it made them shake with fright.

An ugly statue made of gold
stood high above the town.
Its monstrous mouth was open wide,
its evil eyes glared down.

Then messengers rode everywhere
to read the king's new law.
"Hear ye! Hear ye!" they cried aloud
to everyone they saw.
"Whenever people in this land
hear music being played,
they must fall down and pray before
the god our king has made,
or else the king will have you thrown
into a fiery pen."
These words sent shivers up the spines
of even bravest men.

It wasn't long before the sound
of music filled the air,
and all the frightened people fell
upon the ground in prayer.
But suddenly the soldiers cried,
"Why can't we see Meshach?
What's happened to Abednego?
And where is wise Shadrach?"
No one could find them anywhere,
for they had stayed away;
they stayed at home and prayed to God
just as they did each day.

When he found out, the king became
as mad as he could be.
"How dare you disobey my law?"
he asked them angrily.
"Fall down upon your knees at once,
or you will soon be dead!"

But Shadrach
stepped up to the king
and slowly shook his head.
"O King," he said,
"your silly gold
is not a god at all.
It's just a hunk
of ugly junk
outside the city wall.
Our God is very powerful;
He's wise
and strong and true.
And we will pray
to Him each day
no matter what you do."

The king was furious at this—
his face turned white, then red.
"I'll show you I am stronger than
your foolish god," he said.
"Put on their coats! Now tie them up!
And make the fire burn high!"

The red-hot fire grew hotter still;
it reached far in the sky.
Its flames were making roars and howls
so horrible to hear,
the soldiers holding Shadrach and
his friends were filled with fear.
"Now throw them in!" the king called out,
and while they held their breath,
the three brave men fell down,
down,
down,
down to a fiery death.

The flames rose higher now and killed
the soldiers near the pit.
The king and all the people moved
far back away from it.
The fire began to fade away,
and when the smoke had cleared,
the king could not believe his eyes
at what had now appeared.

There in the middle of the flames
four men instead of three
were walking all around the fire
alive as they could be.
The fourth man was an angel sent
by God into the pit;
he guarded so the men had not
been burned one little bit.
The king was so surprised that he
could hardly move or speak;
instead of feeling proud right now,
he felt a little weak.

At last he called, "Abednego,
Shadrach, Meshach, come out.
Why, not one hair is burned!" he said
as they turned round about.
"You truly must be men of God,
for He has set you free.
From this day on you'll be my friends
and rule along with me.
How wonderful your great God is!
Today I do command
that all my people honor Him
throughout my mighty land."

Dear Parents:

The narrative of Shadrach, Meshach, and Abednego is a story of God at work in the lives of people. God gave these three young men a strong faith. They loved and trusted God so much that they were ready to walk in fire rather than deny Him for other gods. Even the powerful king of mighty Babylon could not move them to disobey God. God was at work, keeping them in faith.

God was also at work to protect them from the flames of the fire. He sent His angel messenger to deliver them from burning to death. He used this mighty act of deliverance to lead the king and many people in the land to know Him as the true God over all the earth.

God is also at work in the lives of His people today. He shows His love and power to us in Jesus Christ. In the Gospel God shares with us the good news that Jesus delivered us from all evil by His death on the cross and His resurrection from the grave. God tells us that Jesus overcame temptations to deny His Father and to worship false gods. God sends His Spirit to lead us to faith in Him. He stands by us with His loving power when we are tempted to choose what is popular instead of what is godly, when we are urged to take the easy way instead of the right way as children of God.

Will you help your child appreciate the love of God and His deliverance in Jesus Christ? Will you strengthen your child's faith in the wonderful goodness of God, especially in time of danger and temptation?

The Editor